WRITE THE STORY

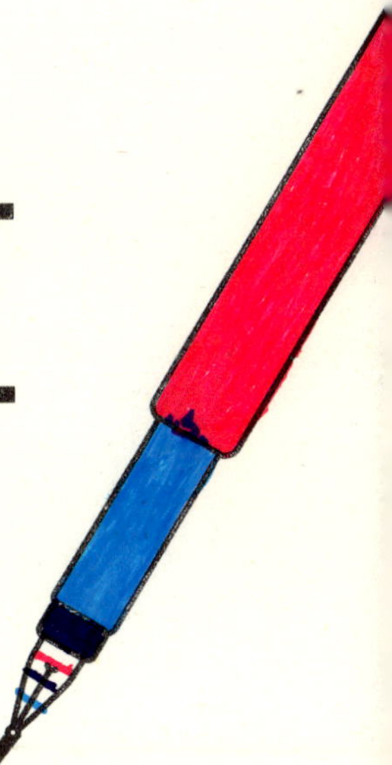

The Year 2563
wander ✦ ex ✦ cavern ✦ motorcycle ✦ jungle ✦ invasion ✦

Lucky Break
tiger ✦ emoticon ✦ wizard ✦ skull ✦ high ✦ foretell ✦

Haunted House
avenue ✦ teenager ✦ leopard ✦ arsenal ✦

Time Travel
fury ✦ seven ✦ constellation ✦ guitar ✦ shipwreck ✦

History Rewritten
rune ✦ moonwalk ✦ alien ✦ cathedral ✦ pizza ✦

Encounter at Sea
library ✦ carnival ✦ secret ✦ telephone ✦ island ✦ roller skate ✦

Unsolved Mystery
sassafras ✦ horse ✦ surprise ✦ yellow ✦ masquerade ✦

This edition published by Piccadilly (USA) Inc.

Piccadilly (USA) Inc.
12702 Via Cortina, Suite 203
Del Mar, CA 92014
USA

10 9 8 7 6 5 4 3 2 1

Designed in California
Made in Vietnam

ISBN-13: 978-1-60863-768-3

Write the Story: **Drama In and Out Of the Lab**

Include the following in your story:

✧ *microbiologist* ✧ *telephone* ✧ *hidden* ✧ *bystander* ✧ *trench*
✧ *inside* ✧ *international* ✧ *shoe* ✧ *heights* ✧ *persuade*

Write the Story: **Chasing the Enemy**

Include the following in your story:

✧ *demon* ✧ *bystander* ✧ *escaped* ✧ *parakeet* ✧ *destiny*
✧ *hammer* ✧ *singing* ✧ *ash* ✧ *cathedral* ✧ *heels*

Write the Story: **An Unexpected Union**

Include the following in your story:

✧ *brothers* ✧ *potato* ✧ *common* ✧ *hands* ✧ *boyfriend*
✧ *alphabet* ✧ *scribble* ✧ *hydrangea* ✧ *sandwich* ✧ *tug-of-war*

Write the Story: **A Lunch Date Gone Wrong**

Include the following in your story:

✧ *eruption* ✧ *salad* ✧ *fire* ✧ *career* ✧ *assume*

✧ *roller skate* ✧ *draw* ✧ *promise* ✧ *full moon* ✧ *sweet*

I was on a date we went, to a ice cream place called "daisy" we sat down

Write the Story: **Business as UNusual**

Include the following in your story:

✧ *housewife* ✧ *moonwalk* ✧ *dog* ✧ *basement* ✧ *conclude*

✧ *alien* ✧ *ignore* ✧ *lightning* ✧ *embrace* ✧ *time*

Write the Story: **The Year Is 2563 ...**

Include the following in your story:

- ✧ *space station*
- ✧ *knuckle*
- ✧ *interview*
- ✧ *horse*
- ✧ *twenty-seven*
- ✧ *lipstick*
- ✧ *transformation*
- ✧ *studio*
- ✧ *distribution*
- ✧ *assert*

Write the Story: **Friends on the Town**

Include the following in your story:

✧ *pizza* ✧ *booth* ✧ *college* ✧ *restore* ✧ *collection*
✧ *rip* ✧ *Buffalo wings* ✧ *chiffon* ✧ *butcher* ✧ *display*

Write the Story: **Today at the Amusement Park**

Include the following in your story:

✧ *Ferris wheel* ✧ *revive* ✧ *dinosaur* ✧ *split* ✧ *disk*

✧ *assumption* ✧ *exceed* ✧ *narrow* ✧ *snickerdoodle* ✧ *join*

Write the Story: **A Day in the Life**

Include the following in your story:

- ✧ *identical*
- ✧ *pot roast*
- ✧ *decorate*
- ✧ *sign*
- ✧ *abuse*
- ✧ *library*
- ✧ *amnesia*
- ✧ *butcher*
- ✧ *submit*
- ✧ *sensation*

Write the Story: **The Last Moment of Childhood**

Include the following in your story:

✧ *Halloween* ✧ *refrigerator* ✧ *pier* ✧ *strengthen* ✧ *voices*

✧ *surprise* ✧ *contribute* ✧ *bird* ✧ *iron* ✧ *requirement*

Write the Story: **Wrapping Up a Business Trip**

Include the following in your story:

✧ *bar* ✧ *laptop* ✧ *insect* ✧ *Germany* ✧ *baseball*

✧ *nervous* ✧ *embark* ✧ *protest* ✧ *swing* ✧ *sentence*

Write the Story: **A Couple on a Cruise**

Include the following in your story:

✧ *nosy* ✧ *sponsor* ✧ *passenger* ✧ *willing* ✧ *smile*

✧ *brew* ✧ *yellow* ✧ *neighbor* ✧ *hundred* ✧ *stairwell*

Write the Story: **Unsolved Mystery**

Include the following in your story:

✧ *murder* ✧ *green* ✧ *agreement* ✧ *traditional* ✧ *carpenter*
✧ *snake* ✧ *sugar* ✧ *kidney* ✧ *congress* ✧ *jam*

Write the Story: **Magic Interferes in New Orleans**

Include the following in your story:

✧ *matriarch* ✧ *throat* ✧ *impossible* ✧ *vinegar* ✧ *apology*

✧ *slice* ✧ *microwave* ✧ *raspberry* ✧ *choose* ✧ *snore*

Write the Story: **A Romantic Scene in an Unromantic Place**

Include the following in your story:

✧ *blacksmith* ✧ *tongue* ✧ *woman* ✧ *spark* ✧ *musical*

✧ *blind* ✧ *Bible* ✧ *barbeque* ✧ *elbow* ✧ *bundle*

Write the Story: **On a Quest**

Include the following in your story:

✧ *medieval* ✧ *derive* ✧ *molten* ✧ *oar* ✧ *rhythm*

✧ *ears* ✧ *antique* ✧ *corn* ✧ *daughter* ✧ *yammer*

Write the Story: **The Supernatural Invades the Everyday**

Include the following in your story:

✧ *metamorphosis* ✧ *rogue* ✧ *shrug* ✧ *salamander* ✧ *sleepy*
✧ *chimpanzee* ✧ *enzyme* ✧ *lemon* ✧ *glance* ✧ *merge*

Write the Story: **A Journalist Crosses the Line**

Include the following in your story:

✧ *defamation* ✧ *stroke* ✧ *reporter* ✧ *truck* ✧ *weasel*
✧ *supermarket* ✧ *encyclopedia* ✧ *contemplate* ✧ *classify* ✧ *clutch*

Write the Story: **Big Time Deals in the Big City**

Include the following in your story:

✧ *feud* ✧ *philosophy* ✧ *palace* ✧ *finger* ✧ *scandal*

✧ *skyscraper* ✧ *complacent* ✧ *handle* ✧ *crawl* ✧ *challenge*

Write the Story: **A Scientist Makes an Unexpected Discovery**

Include the following in your story:

- *parallel*
- *informal*
- *crude*
- *expand*
- *popular*
- *unlikely*
- *analyst*
- *replacement*
- *cell*
- *chest*

Write the Story: **Students Take on a Challenge**

Include the following in your story:

✧ *masquerade* ✧ *gang* ✧ *allege* ✧ *double* ✧ *lucky*

✧ *tea* ✧ *personality* ✧ *introduction* ✧ *parasite* ✧ *class*

Write the Story: **Office Intrigue in the Future**

Include the following in your story:

✧ *time travel* ✧ *trousers* ✧ *supervise* ✧ *successfully* ✧ *law*
✧ *identity* ✧ *mustard* ✧ *kitchen* ✧ *tooth* ✧ *fly*

Write the Story: **Political Machinations**

Include the following in your story:

✧ *appointment* ✧ *dangerous* ✧ *cost* ✧ *empire* ✧ *kitten*
✧ *mug* ✧ *converter* ✧ *essence* ✧ *tennis* ✧ *poke*

Write the Story: **History Rewritten**

Include the following in your story:

✧ *funeral* ✧ *condemn* ✧ *distribution* ✧ *button* ✧ *sink*
✧ *art* ✧ *jealousy* ✧ *brain* ✧ *tax* ✧ *lover*

Write the Story: **On the Campaign Trail**

Include the following in your story:

- *president*
- *dove*
- *tremble*
- *column*
- *united*
- *secretary*
- *impression*
- *soup*
- *milk*
- *armor*

Write the Story: **The Problems of Celebrities**

Include the following in your story:

- *tabloid*
- *existence*
- *dolphin*
- *bunker*
- *surgery*
- *parade*
- *chase*
- *master*
- *smash*
- *possum*

Write the Story: **Tension in Suburbia**

Include the following in your story:

- *muffled*
- *medical*
- *orchid*
- *par*
- *reign*
- *animal*
- *church*
- *shirt*
- *snatch*
- *grin*

Write the Story: **The Gala Event of the Season**

Include the following in your story:

✧ *cater waiter* ✧ *suspicious* ✧ *architecture* ✧ *money* ✧ *switch*
✧ *imagine* ✧ *yawn* ✧ *blot* ✧ *lilac* ✧ *program*

Write the Story: **The Love of Each Other's Lives**

Include the following in your story:

✧ *piano* ✧ *fish* ✧ *store* ✧ *ceiling fan* ✧ *behave*

✧ *breathe* ✧ *describe* ✧ *irritating* ✧ *enthusiastically* ✧ *righteous*

Write the Story: **A Much Needed Vacation**

Include the following in your story:

✧ *hair salon* ✧ *burn* ✧ *escape* ✧ *waste* ✧ *yesterday*

✧ *quack* ✧ *quaint* ✧ *jittery* ✧ *bob* ✧ *expensive*

Write the Story: **A Bartender's Best Night Ever**

Include the following in your story:

✧ *airport* ✧ *appreciate* ✧ *curve* ✧ *grumpy* ✧ *ruthless*

✧ *record* ✧ *nerve* ✧ *acoustics* ✧ *alarm* ✧ *expert*

Write the Story: **A Small, Local Political Race**

Include the following in your story:

✧ *coordinated* ✧ *support* ✧ *farmhand* ✧ *spray* ✧ *serious*
✧ *rail* ✧ *lips* ✧ *taxpayer* ✧ *fool* ✧ *meddler*

Write the Story: **A New Love Blooms in Old Age**

Include the following in your story:

✧ *inheritance* ✧ *walk* ✧ *dust* ✧ *dapper* ✧ *husky*

✧ *squirrel* ✧ *plantation* ✧ *berry* ✧ *silk* ✧ *shovel*

Write the Story: **A Family-Run Farm**

Include the following in your story:

✧ *temporary* ✧ *invent* ✧ *trust* ✧ *horse* ✧ *burst*
✧ *pulley* ✧ *signal* ✧ *dam* ✧ *punch* ✧ *checker*

Write the Story: **A Support Group Meeting**

Include the following in your story:

✧ *novelist* ✧ *fountain* ✧ *snow* ✧ *lady* ✧ *pastoral*

✧ *communicate* ✧ *scene* ✧ *sprout* ✧ *carve* ✧ *whisper*

Write the Story: **Behind The Scenes at the Theater**

Include the following in your story:

✧ *loneliness* ✧ *applaud* ✧ *beg* ✧ *jogging* ✧ *memorize*

✧ *admit* ✧ *solitude* ✧ *converse* ✧ *eternity* ✧ *marsh*

Write the Story: **On Main Street in a Small Town**

Include the following in your story:

- *square*
- *separate*
- *type*
- *truculent*
- *preach*
- *wilderness*
- *pang*
- *façade*
- *pawn*
- *pavement*

Write the Story: **Running Away From Change**

Include the following in your story:

✧ *flight* ✧ *blacktop* ✧ *tense* ✧ *contemplation* ✧ *window*

✧ *enclosure* ✧ *spit* ✧ *blink* ✧ *trade* ✧ *fence*

Write the Story: **A Police Investigation**

Include the following in your story:

- *ominous*
- *arrest*
- *decay*
- *squeal*
- *reduce*
- *feline*
- *avoid*
- *feet*
- *blackberry*
- *bark*

Write the Story: **A Woman's First Day in a Convent**

Include the following in your story:

✧ *nun* ✧ *zealous* ✧ *grateful* ✧ *statue* ✧ *lick*

✧ *attend* ✧ *film* ✧ *page* ✧ *recognize* ✧ *pomegranate*

Write the Story: **A Fishing Trip**

Include the following in your story:

✧ *jig* ✧ *unsightly* ✧ *wait* ✧ *beam* ✧ *shoulder*

✧ *grey* ✧ *reminder* ✧ *mouth* ✧ *Canada* ✧ *river*

Write the Story: **Living with a Chronic Illness**

Include the following in your story:

- *fever*
- *weight*
- *unpack*
- *rollercoaster*
- *surgeon*
- *daffodil*
- *Northern*
- *patch*
- *mossy*
- *tendril*

Write the Story: **Doctors Off Duty**

Include the following in your story:

✧ *goose* ✧ *anatomy* ✧ *Spanish* ✧ *pitcher* ✧ *topography*

✧ *smoke* ✧ *homeward* ✧ *gritty* ✧ *sailor* ✧ *salt*

Write the Story: **Two Best Friends are Baristas**

Include the following in your story:

✧ *coffee* ✧ *molehill* ✧ *insulation* ✧ *sneakers* ✧ *inspire*

✧ *pencil* ✧ *embroidery* ✧ *justify* ✧ *loveless* ✧ *pane*

Write the Story: **A Middle Class Family Doing Its Best**

Include the following in your story:

✧ *castle* ✧ *beetle* ✧ *Facebook* ✧ *calculator* ✧ *nostril*

✧ *timetable* ✧ *wireless* ✧ *stripes* ✧ *scroll* ✧ *white*

Write the Story: **An Intern Meets Someone for Lunch**

Include the following in your story:

✧ *father* ✧ *continent* ✧ *favorite* ✧ *comfortable* ✧ *highlight*
✧ *drive* ✧ *salesman* ✧ *pair* ✧ *mail* ✧ *level*

Write the Story: **A Babysitter Snoops and Finds Something Unexpected**

Include the following in your story:

✧ *newspaper* ✧ *cardinal* ✧ *cotton* ✧ *document* ✧ *tiramisu*

✧ *blackened* ✧ *prediction* ✧ *borderline* ✧ *freedom* ✧ *female*

Write the Story: **A Fortune Cookie Comes True**

Include the following in your story:

✧ *numerology* ✧ *hilarious* ✧ *dictionary* ✧ *recycled* ✧ *brick*
✧ *ocean* ✧ *meaningful* ✧ *garbage* ✧ *star* ✧ *origin*

Write the Story: **Having the Boss Over For Dinner**

Include the following in your story:

✧ *cerulean* ✧ *chair* ✧ *joyous* ✧ *meatloaf* ✧ *pallid*

✧ *brioche* ✧ *monthly* ✧ *thirteen* ✧ *forehead* ✧ *video*

Write the Story: **A Camping Trip in Which No One Has Ever Been Camping Before**

Include the following in your story:

✧ *constellation* ✧ *ketchup* ✧ *royal* ✧ *gear* ✧ *atmosphere*
✧ *expand* ✧ *livid* ✧ *example* ✧ *luminous* ✧ *moonlit*

Write the Story: **The Night Before Graduation**

Include the following in your story:

- ✧ *obscene*
- ✧ *margarita*
- ✧ *paradise*
- ✧ *story*
- ✧ *tempo*
- ✧ *truthfully*
- ✧ *stonewall*
- ✧ *plain*
- ✧ *opposite*
- ✧ *loan*

Write the Story: **A Strange Proposition From a Stranger**

Include the following in your story:

✧ *sequin* ✧ *luncheon* ✧ *designer* ✧ *toolbox* ✧ *measurement*

✧ *force* ✧ *dented* ✧ *cellular* ✧ *banish* ✧ *lock*

Write the Story: **A Mysterious Package**

Include the following in your story:

- *theater*
- *almond*
- *version*
- *triple*
- *arrow*
- *pathway*
- *man*
- *mangle*
- *drapery*
- *bullet*

Write the Story: **Fired From a Long-Term Job**

Include the following in your story:

✧ *guitar* ✧ *military* ✧ *aversion* ✧ *mouse* ✧ *vertical*
✧ *crumple* ✧ *runaway* ✧ *creation* ✧ *alphabetize* ✧ *tablet*

Write the Story: **A New Take on the Arthurian Legend**

Include the following in your story:

✧ *Avalon* ✧ *crossbow* ✧ *orphan* ✧ *list* ✧ *comrade*

✧ *corruption* ✧ *lake* ✧ *enfold* ✧ *disgraceful* ✧ *grass*

Write the Story: **Anonymous Gifts Start Arriving at the Doorstep**

Include the following in your story:

✧ *teenager* ✧ *camouflage* ✧ *birch* ✧ *harmony* ✧ *rifle*
✧ *screen door* ✧ *wrinkle* ✧ *dive* ✧ *pick-up* ✧ *sticker*

Write the Story: **Mash Up Two Classic Fairy Tales into One Story**

Include the following in your story:

✧ *fireplace* ✧ *sword* ✧ *grove* ✧ *stoke* ✧ *underbrush*
✧ *mourn* ✧ *seven* ✧ *friendship* ✧ *cardboard* ✧ *giver*

Write the Story: **A Missionary in a Remote Village**

Include the following in your story:

✧ *orchestra* ✧ *finch* ✧ *aim* ✧ *development* ✧ *ex*

✧ *bold* ✧ *old-fashioned* ✧ *gut* ✧ *brassy* ✧ *sharp*

Write the Story: **A Teenager Whose Parents Have Unwelcome News**

Include the following in your story:

✧ *comic book* ✧ *battery* ✧ *crumbly* ✧ *apartment* ✧ *angelic*
✧ *breach* ✧ *shooter* ✧ *soda* ✧ *engineer* ✧ *substantiate*

Write the Story: **A Shooting in a Public Place**

Include the following in your story:

✧ *shipwreck* ✧ *pummel* ✧ *nurse* ✧ *structure* ✧ *home*
✧ *offset* ✧ *cabin* ✧ *puppy* ✧ *knot* ✧ *tide*

Write the Story: **Picking Up a Hitchhiker**

Include the following in your story:

✧ *hospital* ✧ *defer* ✧ *interface* ✧ *experiment* ✧ *beaker*
✧ *visualize* ✧ *mattress* ✧ *skyline* ✧ *interpret* ✧ *zap*

Write the Story: **Selling a Childhood Home**

Include the following in your story:

✧ *dreamscape* ✧ *convince* ✧ *pioneer* ✧ *genesis* ✧ *cumulous*

✧ *jump* ✧ *mash* ✧ *condition* ✧ *erase* ✧ *gold*

I sat by my bedroom window as

Write the Story: **A Wild Animal Loose in the House**

Include the following in your story:

✧ *pregnant* ✧ *community* ✧ *logo* ✧ *statistics* ✧ *democracy*
✧ *honesty* ✧ *criminal* ✧ *ankle* ✧ *orange* ✧ *comment*

Write the Story: **A Midlife Career Change**

Include the following in your story:

- *chef*
- *upgrade*
- *monkey*
- *turkey*
- *fashion*
- *team*
- *harden*
- *noon*
- *elevator*
- *baste*

Write the Story: **A Ghost Story**

Include the following in your story:

- *tango*
- *diversify*
- *blog*
- *invisible*
- *missile*
- *glitter*
- *scuff*
- *balloon*
- *bird cage*
- *grizzly bear*

Write the Story: **The Main Character Thinks He or She is About to Get Fired**

Include the following in your story:

- ✧ *magazine*
- ✧ *blow-dryer*
- ✧ *congeal*
- ✧ *bluebell*
- ✧ *cummerbund*
- ✧ *wheelie bag*
- ✧ *pastels*
- ✧ *cheeseburger*
- ✧ *binding*
- ✧ *science*

Write the Story: **A Coastal Town in New England is Full of Crazy Characters**

Include the following in your story:

✧ *lobsterman* ✧ *bicycle* ✧ *light bulb* ✧ *yoga* ✧ *fireworks*

✧ *infantile* ✧ *weave* ✧ *leopard* ✧ *balding* ✧ *sunset*

Write the Story: **A Haunted House**

Include the following in your story:

✧ *silver* ✧ *relativity* ✧ *watercolor* ✧ *Copper Beech* ✧ *limited*
✧ *affect* ✧ *broccoli* ✧ *politician* ✧ *arsenal* ✧ *cufflink*

Write the Story: **Something Bad is About to Happen, But Nobody Believes the Main Character**

Include the following in your story:

✧ *Andromeda* ✧ *stop sign* ✧ *dandelion* ✧ *iceberg* ✧ *spectacle*
✧ *poet* ✧ *candle lit* ✧ *keyboard* ✧ *bumble* ✧ *robotic*

Write the Story: **A Writer with Noisy Neighbors**

Include the following in your story:

✧ *dentist* ✧ *rainbow* ✧ *explosion* ✧ *horizon* ✧ *cactus*

✧ *palm* ✧ *Saturday* ✧ *latte* ✧ *beets* ✧ *sample*

Write the Story: **Newlyweds on Their Honeymoon**

Include the following in your story:

✧ *cockpit* ✧ *selfie* ✧ *kayak* ✧ *thought bubble* ✧ *picnic table*

✧ *wander* ✧ *propose* ✧ *shiatsu* ✧ *motherhood* ✧ *temple*

Write the Story: **The Main Character Goes on a Trip Alone to Gain Perspective**

Include the following in your story:

✧ *lighthouse* ✧ *flock* ✧ *muscle* ✧ *sprinkle* ✧ *insult*
✧ *cliffhanger* ✧ *cheetah* ✧ *chartreuse* ✧ *wrist* ✧ *seedling*

Write the Story: **A Character with OCD in the Worst Possible Situation**

Include the following in your story:

✧ *monastery* ✧ *chalkboard* ✧ *elephant* ✧ *coast* ✧ *turmeric*

✧ *poppy* ✧ *defeat* ✧ *chessboard* ✧ *inhumane* ✧ *search*

Write the Story: **An Alien in Disguise Among Humans**

Include the following in your story:

✧ *Aurora Borealis* ✧ *paint brush* ✧ *corn field* ✧ *cluster* ✧ *lineup*
✧ *overlook* ✧ *suspect* ✧ *bridge* ✧ *dome* ✧ *dash*

Write the Story: **A Young Child Makes a Discovery**

Include the following in your story:

✧ *Superman* ✧ *ginkgo biloba* ✧ *cavern* ✧ *clicker* ✧ *aloe*

✧ *moviegoer* ✧ *stretch* ✧ *furry* ✧ *yardstick* ✧ *makeup*

Write the Story: **High School Hierarchy**

Include the following in your story:

✧ *pyramid* ✧ *cowboy hat* ✧ *amateurish* ✧ *angle* ✧ *ripple*

✧ *cheese* ✧ *jersey* ✧ *blister* ✧ *odyssey* ✧ *reorder*

Write the Story: **The Main Character has Amnesia**

Include the following in your story:

- *antiquarian*
- *satellite*
- *cinnamon*
- *fortune*
- *cookie*
- *harbor*
- *cedar*
- *invitation*
- *soccer*
- *annual*
- *speaker*

Write the Story: **The Early Days of the Zombie Apocalypse**

Include the following in your story:

✧ *motherboard* ✧ *buffalo* ✧ *Eiffel Tower* ✧ *raven* ✧ *motorcycle*
✧ *envelope* ✧ *tulip* ✧ *moon* ✧ *reflect* ✧ *sycamore*

Write the Story: **Adult Friends on Vacation in the Tropics**

Include the following in your story:

✧ *scuba diver* ✧ *champagne* ✧ *invasion* ✧ *archway* ✧ *hoard*
✧ *strawberry* ✧ *penguin* ✧ *autumnal* ✧ *cease* ✧ *mist*

Write the Story: **The Main Character Thwarts Traditional Gender Roles**

Include the following in your story:

- *woman*
- *bestseller*
- *buttress*
- *goldfish*
- *barnyard*
- *walkway*
- *crop*
- *winter*
- *driveway*
- *steer*

Write the Story: **Memory Editing Wreaks Havoc**

Include the following in your story:

✧ *Jupiter* ✧ *chocolate* ✧ *domestic* ✧ *blossom* ✧ *ladder*

✧ *steam* ✧ *extension* ✧ *pine cone* ✧ *sunrise* ✧ *tide*

Write the Story: **A Tour Guide in the Florida Keys**

Include the following in your story:

- *revolver*
- *headphones*
- *doughnut*
- *leopard*
- *spaghetti*
- *tiki hut*
- *magma*
- *magnetize*
- *swampy*
- *recital*

Write the Story: **A Dystopian Glimpse of the Future**

Include the following in your story:

✧ *wheelchair* ✧ *Labrador* ✧ *throne* ✧ *jungle* ✧ *prescription*
✧ *railroad* ✧ *trunk* ✧ *gulley* ✧ *wasp* ✧ *photosynthesize*

Write the Story: **A Letter Changes Everything**

Include the following in your story:

✧ *alchemist* ✧ *waterfall* ✧ *birthday* ✧ *cottage* ✧ *spring*
✧ *roar* ✧ *syrup* ✧ *sift* ✧ *immeasurable* ✧ *bank*

Write the Story: **Getting Away with Murder**

Include the following in your story:

✧ *Snow Queen* ✧ *windmill* ✧ *tunnel* ✧ *childhood* ✧ *endanger*

✧ *cypress* ✧ *wine* ✧ *horseback* ✧ *temperature* ✧ *imperial*

Write the Story: **A Sales Manager Has Had Enough**

Include the following in your story:

- *Australia*
- *faith*
- *gullet*
- *customer*
- *butterfly*
- *headlight*
- *badger*
- *shoreline*
- *mountain*
- *owl*

Write the Story: **Something Believed to Be Myth is Very Real**

Include the following in your story:

✧ *necromancer* ✧ *elm* ✧ *roadmap* ✧ *GPS* ✧ *outside*

✧ *twine* ✧ *water lily* ✧ *plastic* ✧ *chopper* ✧ *powerless*

Write the Story: **Based on a True Story**

Include the following in your story:

- *Mongols*
- *exception*
- *gosling*
- *elementary*
- *coordinate*
- *solution*
- *tighten*
- *shuffle*
- *horseshoe*
- *universe*

Write the Story: **Reliving Childhood Memories as an Adult**

Include the following in your story:

✧ *target practice* ✧ *bookmark* ✧ *wizard* ✧ *determination* ✧ *unbridled*
✧ *schedule* ✧ *forward* ✧ *pork loin* ✧ *innermost* ✧ *supposition*

Write the Story: **A Story Pulled From Today's Headlines and Rewritten**

Include the following in your story:

✧ *boxer* ✧ *cherry blossom* ✧ *magic* ✧ *implement* ✧ *artwork*

✧ *safety* ✧ *chime* ✧ *chain link* ✧ *towel* ✧ *ingredient*

Write the Story: **The Villain is Really the Hero**

Include the following in your story:

✧ *witchcraft* ✧ *recommend* ✧ *sand dollar* ✧ *fisticuff* ✧ *paprika*
✧ *eyeball* ✧ *nightlight* ✧ *gibberish* ✧ *infuriating* ✧ *dreadful*

Write the Story: **The Main Character Has Woken Up Missing One of the Five Senses**

Include the following in your story:

✧ *piracy* ✧ *parking* ✧ *seashell* ✧ *selfish* ✧ *adjustment*
✧ *lax* ✧ *slumber* ✧ *fragrance* ✧ *saltine* ✧ *top hat*

Write the Story: **A Story Told Through Emails**

Include the following in your story:

✧ *philanthropist* ✧ *symmetrical* ✧ *terminate* ✧ *noodle* ✧ *emoticon*
✧ *reference* ✧ *sunglasses* ✧ *moonlight* ✧ *borrow* ✧ *newsletter*

Write the Story: **Parents Solve a Problem Together**

Include the following in your story:

✧ *rhinoceros* ✧ *umbrella* ✧ *announcement* ✧ *petal* ✧ *feather*
✧ *fruit* ✧ *placemat* ✧ *sketch* ✧ *wobble* ✧ *boil*

Write the Story: **An Alligator on the Loose**

Include the following in your story:

✧ *New York City* ✧ *Chewbacca* ✧ *typical* ✧ *beard* ✧ *walkabout*
✧ *interrupt* ✧ *clang* ✧ *belly* ✧ *cockatoo* ✧ *stroll*

Write the Story: **Magic in Everyday Occurences**

Include the following in your story:

✧ *Krav Maga* ✧ *touch screen* ✧ *litter* ✧ *vendor* ✧ *doorbell*

✧ *finish* ✧ *hungry* ✧ *aversion* ✧ *signature* ✧ *sweatband*

Write the Story: **A Story That Takes Place in One Room**

Include the following in your story:

✧ *petting zoo* ✧ *handsome* ✧ *unbound* ✧ *annoy* ✧ *weekend*
✧ *invest* ✧ *immortal* ✧ *piglet* ✧ *cocktail* ✧ *camp*

Write the Story: **An Unexpected Visitor Shakes Things Up**

Include the following in your story:

✧ *tightrope* ✧ *nightingale* ✧ *underline* ✧ *risk* ✧ *academy*
✧ *existential* ✧ *outlook* ✧ *Friday* ✧ *gobble* ✧ *grill*

Write the Story: **A Hairdresser Received a Shocking Confession from a Customer**

Include the following in your story:

✧ *poverty* ✧ *marksman* ✧ *bookshelf* ✧ *backspace* ✧ *hedge*

✧ *cuckoo* ✧ *pumpkin* ✧ *courteous* ✧ *deduction* ✧ *acute*

Write the Story: **War on Foreign Soil**

Include the following in your story:

✧ *amputated* ✧ *global* ✧ *curtain* ✧ *banana* ✧ *carbonate*

✧ *calisthenics* ✧ *patriot* ✧ *walnut* ✧ *fixture* ✧ *bluetooth*

Write the Story: **A Conversation Between Artists**

Include the following in your story:

✧ *skull* ✧ *galaxy* ✧ *expression* ✧ *trash can* ✧ *deployment*

✧ *visitor* ✧ *brushstroke* ✧ *decade* ✧ *forgot* ✧ *ponder*

Write the Story: **A Dinner Party**

Include the following in your story:

✧ *phoenix* ✧ *canvas* ✧ *homesick* ✧ *evening* ✧ *spicy*

✧ *rooftop* ✧ *cicada* ✧ *orthodox* ✧ *ding* ✧ *spruce*

Write the Story: **A Night at the Opera**

Include the following in your story:

- ✧ *Air Force*
- ✧ *crane*
- ✧ *orchestrate*
- ✧ *leotard*
- ✧ *stubble*
- ✧ *pinpoint*
- ✧ *placate*
- ✧ *machete*
- ✧ *photo*
- ✧ *pivot*

Write the Story: **A Suspected Affair**

Include the following in your story:

✧ *marriage* ✧ *checklist* ✧ *songbird* ✧ *mango* ✧ *ranch*

✧ *stroke* ✧ *magpie* ✧ *scowl* ✧ *simper* ✧ *commotion*

Write the Story: **Conspiracy Theorists Convention**

Include the following in your story:

✧ *crop circles* ✧ *vacation* ✧ *possum* ✧ *filibuster* ✧ *mutiny*

✧ *scour* ✧ *compass* ✧ *drift* ✧ *drawback* ✧ *electric*

Write the Story: **The Main Character Witnesses a Crime**

Include the following in your story:

✧ *Christmas* ✧ *almond* ✧ *paisley* ✧ *lion* ✧ *pipe*
✧ *scream* ✧ *fade* ✧ *French horn* ✧ *inflate* ✧ *maple*

Write the Story: **The Loss of a Loved One**

Include the following in your story:

✧ *bachelor* ✧ *chandelier* ✧ *ladybug* ✧ *Muslim* ✧ *strive*
✧ *inverse* ✧ *mannerism* ✧ *balance* ✧ *overreact* ✧ *prime*

Write the Story: **A Lucky Break**

Include the following in your story:

✧ *City Hall* ✧ *feminist* ✧ *myth* ✧ *interpreter* ✧ *maverick*
✧ *raccoon* ✧ *radiant* ✧ *scram* ✧ *off switch* ✧ *logic*

Write the Story: **Tumultuous Soulmates are on Opposing Sides of a Conflict**

Include the following in your story:

✧ *apothecary* ✧ *bow tie* ✧ *ladylike* ✧ *sprocket* ✧ *mushroom*

✧ *scrounge* ✧ *frenzy* ✧ *match* ✧ *oust* ✧ *prisoner*

Write the Story: **An Interrupted Journey**

Include the following in your story:

✧ *butterfly effect* ✧ *vulture* ✧ *cramp* ✧ *industry* ✧ *purge*
✧ *scruple* ✧ *snorkel* ✧ *snitch* ✧ *warning* ✧ *unless*

Write the Story: **A Hike Through the Woods**

Include the following in your story:

✧ *leprechaun* ✧ *covert* ✧ *fireball* ✧ *snoop* ✧ *wart*

✧ *pity* ✧ *backpack* ✧ *practice* ✧ *nausea* ✧ *collar*

Write the Story: **The Best Night the Main Character Won't Remember**

Include the following in your story:

✧ *Mardi Gras* ✧ *puzzle* ✧ *scorpion* ✧ *snout* ✧ *ward*

✧ *cooler* ✧ *shake* ✧ *tiger* ✧ *exhausted* ✧ *stumble*

Write the Story: **An Anthropologist at a Costume Party**

Include the following in your story:

✧ *fashionista* ✧ *responsibility* ✧ *cruelty* ✧ *article* ✧ *arrangement*

✧ *frog* ✧ *french fries* ✧ *calf* ✧ *braid* ✧ *addition*

Write the Story: **A Crime Scene**

Include the following in your story:

✧ *phantom* ✧ *desperate* ✧ *scale* ✧ *normality* ✧ *ponytail*
✧ *tremendous* ✧ *stiletto* ✧ *hound* ✧ *wrinkle* ✧ *smoke*

Write the Story: **A Countdown**

Include the following in your story:

- *plumber*
- *witty*
- *oyster*
- *voluntary*
- *asparagus*
- *centralize*
- *judge*
- *puddle*
- *pointer*
- *ampersand*

Write the Story: **A Child's Dream Literally Comes True**

Include the following in your story:

✧ *high school* ✧ *captivate* ✧ *portfolio* ✧ *argyle* ✧ *witness*
✧ *fertile* ✧ *eyebrow* ✧ *pentagram* ✧ *thirsty* ✧ *guidance*

Write the Story: **Stranded in a Foreign City**

Include the following in your story:

✧ *baptist* ✧ *assets* ✧ *cupcake* ✧ *showcase* ✧ *neurology*
✧ *workaday* ✧ *pine* ✧ *cushion* ✧ *assistant* ✧ *firmament*

Write the Story: **A Spy on the Job**

Include the following in your story:

✧ *apostle* ✧ *kitty* ✧ *myriad* ✧ *investment* ✧ *republic*
✧ *crimson* ✧ *flint* ✧ *postern* ✧ *original* ✧ *field*

Write the Story: **In The Middle of a Long, Cold Winter**

Include the following in your story:

✧ *opera* ✧ *redeem* ✧ *razor* ✧ *lungs* ✧ *grace*
✧ *futuristic* ✧ *tread* ✧ *vest* ✧ *milkshake* ✧ *powder*

Write the Story: **Something Valuable Has Been Stolen**

Include the following in your story:

✧ *huntress* ✧ *machinations* ✧ *trophy* ✧ *turncoat* ✧ *treasure*
✧ *minute* ✧ *nook* ✧ *historic* ✧ *rock* ✧ *ruin*

Write the Story: **A Famous Fictional Character in the Wrong Story**

Include the following in your story:

- *stock market*
- *serial*
- *tangy*
- *panda*
- *ensemble*
- *salute*
- *average*
- *Venus*
- *boss*
- *knee*

Write the Story: **A Talented Musician Struggles to Make It Big**

Include the following in your story:

✧ *crocodile* ✧ *anchor* ✧ *lasagna* ✧ *anthem* ✧ *fingernail*

✧ *trout* ✧ *federal* ✧ *bog* ✧ *jostle* ✧ *repel*

Write the Story: **A Family Gathering on a Holiday**

Include the following in your story:

✧ *rabbi* ✧ *irony* ✧ *bamboozle* ✧ *sturgeon* ✧ *bale*

✧ *reserve* ✧ *vanquish* ✧ *submerge* ✧ *plum* ✧ *rhetorical*

Write the Story: **The Main Character Ignored the Warning Label**

Include the following in your story:

✧ *comedian* ✧ *commission* ✧ *trump* ✧ *bamboo* ✧ *bombastic*
✧ *vast* ✧ *blonde* ✧ *gross* ✧ *sophisticated* ✧ *giraffe*

Write the Story: **Conversation on a Train**

Include the following in your story:

✧ *unicorn* ✧ *enslave* ✧ *steak* ✧ *maw* ✧ *plunge*

✧ *worthy* ✧ *recoil* ✧ *absolve* ✧ *suspenders* ✧ *worldwide*

Write the Story: **The Phone Rings at 3 A.M.**

Include the following in your story:

✧ *guerilla* ✧ *emerald* ✧ *careless* ✧ *traffic* ✧ *liberate*
✧ *adolescence* ✧ *punch* ✧ *wave* ✧ *environment* ✧ *oval*

Write the Story: **The Characters Are Aware That They're Fictional**

Include the following in your story:

✧ *oil rig* ✧ *dynasty* ✧ *lousy* ✧ *vault* ✧ *discharge*

✧ *supreme* ✧ *migrate* ✧ *harvest* ✧ *jaw* ✧ *pudding*

Write the Story: **Two People Who Hate Each Other Have to Cooperate**

Include the following in your story:

✧ *kidnap* ✧ *pinstripe* ✧ *quagmire* ✧ *lofty* ✧ *Adirondack*
✧ *pinky* ✧ *aftermath* ✧ *kernel* ✧ *legacy* ✧ *fail*

Write the Story: **The Story Begins at a Funeral**

Include the following in your story:

✧ *poker* ✧ *paramount* ✧ *earlobe* ✧ *marrow* ✧ *epic*
✧ *upgrade* ✧ *offshoot* ✧ *chihuahua* ✧ *episode* ✧ *icon*

Write the Story: **Five People from Completely Different Backgrounds Seated Together**

Include the following in your story:

✧ *Vietnam* ✧ *stakes* ✧ *sequel* ✧ *club* ✧ *lens*

✧ *draft* ✧ *perpetual* ✧ *otherwise* ✧ *groom* ✧ *hidden*

Write the Story: **Time Travel**

Include the following in your story:

✧ *hurricane* ✧ *email* ✧ *launder* ✧ *pastry* ✧ *garlic*
✧ *staff* ✧ *germs* ✧ *gallery* ✧ *brace* ✧ *share*

Write the Story: **Someone is Hiding in the Linen Closet**

Include the following in your story:

- *grandfather*
- *canoe*
- *pear*
- *cakewalk*
- *blouse*
- *assignment*
- *stampede*
- *present*
- *dinner*
- *slurp*

Write the Story: **A Deal with the Devil**

Include the following in your story:

✧ *regime* ✧ *album* ✧ *torch* ✧ *lodge* ✧ *highway*

✧ *sandy* ✧ *rune* ✧ *contract* ✧ *token* ✧ *suit*

Write the Story: **A Priest Hearing a Unique Confession**

Include the following in your story:

✧ *Chinese* ✧ *crustacean* ✧ *flash* ✧ *bucket* ✧ *vessel*

✧ *notice* ✧ *memoir* ✧ *brute* ✧ *docile* ✧ *cucumber*

Write the Story: **The Main Character is Startled Awake By ...**

Include the following in your story:

✧ *subway* ✧ *evergreen* ✧ *core* ✧ *emblem* ✧ *wild*
✧ *swine* ✧ *poised* ✧ *occupation* ✧ *inspector* ✧ *gate*

Write the Story: **Escaping a Natural Disaster**

Include the following in your story:

✧ *museum* ✧ *exonerate* ✧ *epicurean* ✧ *senseless* ✧ *literacy*
✧ *software* ✧ *solar* ✧ *tear* ✧ *coloring* ✧ *quarry*

Write the Story: **A Blind Date**

Include the following in your story:

- ✧ *park bench* ✧ *manager* ✧ *beastie* ✧ *honeydew* ✧ *justice*
- ✧ *manmade* ✧ *placement* ✧ *fabric* ✧ *prevention* ✧ *basket*

Write the Story: **A Hermit Is Forced to Go to a Crowded Place**

Include the following in your story:

✧ *typewriter* ✧ *water bottle* ✧ *lenient* ✧ *clerk* ✧ *render*
✧ *runner* ✧ *soil* ✧ *sewn* ✧ *chauffeur* ✧ *waterway*

Write the Story: **Caught in the Rain**

Include the following in your story:

✧ *Las Vegas* ✧ *radiology* ✧ *etch* ✧ *funeral* ✧ *textile*

✧ *sweep* ✧ *muslin* ✧ *wholesale* ✧ *wildlife* ✧ *English*

Write the Story: **A Couple Who Married Young**

Include the following in your story:

✧ *Monopoly* ✧ *flashlight* ✧ *aerospace* ✧ *exchange* ✧ *biology*
✧ *lawyer* ✧ *machinery* ✧ *revenge* ✧ *anthill* ✧ *concealed*

Write the Story: **A Myth That Explains a Common Natural Occurrence**

Include the following in your story:

✧ *river mouth* ✧ *punishment* ✧ *warehouse* ✧ *claim* ✧ *coder*
✧ *ache* ✧ *bend* ✧ *coop* ✧ *dam* ✧ *frown*

Write the Story: **A Nasty Rumor**

Include the following in your story:

✧ *Antarctica* ✧ *candy bar* ✧ *sympathetic* ✧ *minister* ✧ *patrol*
✧ *commonality* ✧ *auction* ✧ *bandage* ✧ *crush* ✧ *dive*

Write the Story: **A Lifelong Bachelor Visiting Married Friends**

Include the following in your story:

✧ *tick tock* ✧ *factory* ✧ *zoology* ✧ *arrest* ✧ *broadcast*

✧ *comb* ✧ *divorce* ✧ *flap* ✧ *harness* ✧ *gaze*

Write the Story: **A Mistake That Costs Someone's Life**

Include the following in your story:

✧ *Everglades* ✧ *bulletin* ✧ *fiend* ✧ *crew* ✧ *floss*

✧ *humor* ✧ *grease* ✧ *kiss* ✧ *link* ✧ *notice*

Write the Story: **A Good Reason to Be Afraid of the Dark**

Include the following in your story:

✧ *killer whale* ✧ *depraved* ✧ *janitor* ✧ *bargain* ✧ *dye*
✧ *fool* ✧ *heap* ✧ *kick* ✧ *praise* ✧ *quilt*

Write the Story: **Alone on a Deserted Island**

Include the following in your story:

✧ *book review* ✧ *organism* ✧ *mermaid* ✧ *bother* ✧ *decrease*
✧ *echo* ✧ *grimace* ✧ *inch* ✧ *march* ✧ *pump*

Write the Story: **A Fairy Tale in a Faraway Land**

Include the following in your story:

- *dragon*
- *strike*
- *collection*
- *guess*
- *joke*
- *smirk*
- *twist*
- *upstage*
- *wreck*
- *beaver*

Write the Story: **The Main Character Gets Rejected**

Include the following in your story:

✧ *office* ✧ *popcorn* ✧ *genial* ✧ *rhyme* ✧ *shampoo*
✧ *vote* ✧ *yawn* ✧ *baboon* ✧ *freak* ✧ *hag*

Write the Story: **A Divorced Couple is Stuck Together**

Include the following in your story:

✧ *twister* ✧ *specialist* ✧ *grate* ✧ *swivel* ✧ *elk*

✧ *arise* ✧ *assertive* ✧ *torment* ✧ *zest* ✧ *solvent*

Write the Story: **An Anniversary Party**

Include the following in your story:

✧ *tour guide* ✧ *sprout* ✧ *beluga* ✧ *breed* ✧ *galoshes*

✧ *bitterness* ✧ *adversary* ✧ *binary* ✧ *radiant* ✧ *transit*

Write the Story: **A Difficult Decision**

Include the following in your story:

- *Grand Canyon*
- *skate*
- *vacuum*
- *waltz*
- *grizzly*
- *cling*
- *brogue*
- *agony*
- *twinkling*
- *observatory*

Write the Story: **The Cast of a Broadway Show**

Include the following in your story:

✧ *gargoyle* ✧ *advertisement* ✧ *shelter* ✧ *cast* ✧ *calculating*
✧ *singularity* ✧ *dwarf* ✧ *arithmetic* ✧ *rubber* ✧ *scissors*

Write the Story: **A Summer Job**

Include the following in your story:

✧ *amusement park* ✧ *unrefined* ✧ *silence* ✧ *tease* ✧ *creep*

✧ *elated* ✧ *interstellar* ✧ *spiral* ✧ *quiz* ✧ *agent*

Write the Story: **Grandparents Acting Like Children**

Include the following in your story:

✧ *wedding* ✧ *squash* ✧ *dream* ✧ *foretell* ✧ *gluestick*
✧ *urchin* ✧ *solstice* ✧ *inertia* ✧ *ice* ✧ *composer*

Write the Story: **Keeping a Promise**

Include the following in your story:

✧ *abolitionist* ✧ *coyote* ✧ *forbid* ✧ *gloomy* ✧ *keen*
✧ *lesson* ✧ *genetics* ✧ *variable* ✧ *retort* ✧ *mass*

Write the Story: **Ten People in a Blackout**

Include the following in your story:

✧ *ballet* ✧ *thunder* ✧ *grind* ✧ *handwriting* ✧ *partner*
✧ *yardstick* ✧ *adopt* ✧ *swarm* ✧ *bundle* ✧ *prodigious*

Write the Story: **Shenanigans on a Movie Set**

Include the following in your story:

✧ *stunt* ✧ *wring* ✧ *lull* ✧ *stingy* ✧ *husband*

✧ *ginger* ✧ *buggy* ✧ *pedal* ✧ *llama* ✧ *anaconda*

Write the Story: **A Coup at a Secret Base**

Include the following in your story:

✧ *desert* ✧ *waylay* ✧ *pensive* ✧ *gazillions* ✧ *juniper*

✧ *helicopter* ✧ *lotus* ✧ *captain* ✧ *bandana* ✧ *taco*

Write the Story: **Halloween Night in a Hospital**

Include the following in your story:

✧ *centaur* ✧ *interweave* ✧ *placid* ✧ *benefactor* ✧ *peppermint*
✧ *gondola* ✧ *lambada* ✧ *twilight* ✧ *inlet* ✧ *throw*

Write the Story: **A Comedy of Errors**

Include the following in your story:

✧ *undead* ✧ *shrink* ✧ *quarrelsome* ✧ *harpy* ✧ *rickshaw*
✧ *limbo* ✧ *dusk* ✧ *cricket* ✧ *sunshine* ✧ *whoops*

Write the Story: **An Amateur Film Competition**

Include the following in your story:

✧ *asteroid* ✧ *multitude* ✧ *bobsled* ✧ *rodent* ✧ *boysenberry*

✧ *gut* ✧ *reel* ✧ *showtime* ✧ *buoy* ✧ *spider*

Write the Story: **An EMT Jinxes His/Herself by Hoping for a Quiet Shift**

Include the following in your story:

✧ *ambulance* ✧ *hamster* ✧ *schooner* ✧ *cane* ✧ *whiz*

✧ *outdoors* ✧ *euphoria* ✧ *cylindrical* ✧ *crisp* ✧ *painting*

Write the Story: **Last Call at a Bar in a Big City**

Include the following in your story:

✧ *doppelganger* ✧ *platypus* ✧ *jazz* ✧ *alienated* ✧ *bikini*
✧ *constitution* ✧ *batter* ✧ *temper* ✧ *basin* ✧ *rift*

Write the Story: **A Creature Feature in Present Day**

Include the following in your story:

✧ *werewolf* ✧ *barge* ✧ *caramel* ✧ *housefly* ✧ *awesome*

✧ *simmer* ✧ *analogy* ✧ *gulf* ✧ *femur* ✧ *amber*

Write the Story: **The Crew of a Commercial Fishing Boat**

Include the following in your story:

- ✧ *battleship*
- ✧ *whoosh*
- ✧ *colossal*
- ✧ *vertebrae*
- ✧ *salmon*
- ✧ *mahogany*
- ✧ *paddle*
- ✧ *breakfast*
- ✧ *gathering*
- ✧ *wheel*

Write the Story: **A Single Parent Solves a Problem**

Include the following in your story:

✧ *adoption* ✧ *grotesque* ✧ *cove* ✧ *snail* ✧ *olive*

✧ *navel* ✧ *rivulet* ✧ *hollow* ✧ *ambrosia* ✧ *pale*

Write the Story: **Blast from the Past**

Include the following in your story:

✧ *shrew* ✧ *happy-go-lucky* ✧ *esophagus* ✧ *handkerchief* ✧ *shred*
✧ *clause* ✧ *scone* ✧ *pewter* ✧ *biscuit* ✧ *necklace*

Write the Story: **A Dog Walker in Washington, DC**

Include the following in your story:

✧ *senator* ✧ *grotto* ✧ *strudel* ✧ *jade* ✧ *welcome*

✧ *slang* ✧ *complementary* ✧ *vacant* ✧ *jellyfish* ✧ *admonish*

Write the Story: **An Interview on Live TV**

Include the following in your story:

✧ *bishop* ✧ *impish* ✧ *amoeba* ✧ *sheep* ✧ *denim*

✧ *jet* ✧ *apricot* ✧ *sepia* ✧ *nipple* ✧ *bellow*

Write the Story: **It's a Setup!**

Include the following in your story:

✧ *acrobat* ✧ *blurt* ✧ *jolt* ✧ *gregarious* ✧ *tortoise*

✧ *persimmon* ✧ *balk* ✧ *follow* ✧ *gasp* ✧ *deli*

Write the Story: **Be Careful What You Wish For**

Include the following in your story:

✧ *toadstool* ✧ *bluff* ✧ *yodel* ✧ *thistle* ✧ *smock*

✧ *rust* ✧ *tomato* ✧ *bestow* ✧ *enunciate* ✧ *medium*

Write the Story: **A Hairbrained Scheme**

Include the following in your story:

✧ *entrepreneur* ✧ *vermilion* ✧ *hazmat* ✧ *bless* ✧ *cashier*
✧ *horseradish* ✧ *banjo* ✧ *melt* ✧ *modify* ✧ *woozy*

Write the Story: **Starting Over in a New Place**

Include the following in your story:

- *Dubai*
- *fedora*
- *sienna*
- *befriend*
- *grate*
- *listen*
- *heiress*
- *twinge*
- *mute*
- *charcoal*

Write the Story: **Tea Time in an English Inn**

Include the following in your story:

✧ *vampire* ✧ *tiara* ✧ *badlands* ✧ *brag* ✧ *empty*

✧ *mauve* ✧ *winged* ✧ *trillion* ✧ *axis* ✧ *cone*

Write the Story: **Right Under Their Noses**

Include the following in your story:

- *catamaran*
- *kaleidoscope*
- *barter*
- *sandcastle*
- *divide*
- *organ*
- *formula*
- *binocular*
- *lecture*
- *ivory*

Write the Story: **Cleaning the Attic Brings Back Memories**

Include the following in your story:

✧ *extravaganza* ✧ *watershed* ✧ *cajole* ✧ *zealous* ✧ *factor*

✧ *teal* ✧ *loosen* ✧ *whistle* ✧ *ogle* ✧ *lemonade*

Write the Story: **A Hostage Situation**

Include the following in your story:

✧ *Hawaiian* ✧ *growl* ✧ *kazoo* ✧ *pledge* ✧ *licorice*

✧ *karate* ✧ *lapel* ✧ *plug* ✧ *terracotta* ✧ *trickle*

Write the Story: **The New Chef's First Day on the Job**

Include the following in your story:

✧ *sultan* ✧ *pause* ✧ *scatter* ✧ *khaki* ✧ *sip*

✧ *undress* ✧ *waver* ✧ *marmalade* ✧ *snare* ✧ *ring*

Write the Story: **An Object Found in the Trash**

Include the following in your story:

✧ *cobbler* ✧ *umber* ✧ *haunt* ✧ *grumble* ✧ *raincoat*

✧ *unleavened* ✧ *bravery* ✧ *ray* ✧ *toffee* ✧ *imaginary*

Write the Story: **A New Life on a New Planet**

Include the following in your story:

✧ *negotiation* ✧ *churro* ✧ *postulate* ✧ *reiterate* ✧ *pullover*
✧ *contentment* ✧ *watermelon* ✧ *beech* ✧ *momentary* ✧ *frozen*

Write the Story: **An Encounter at Sea**

Include the following in your story:

✧ *commodore* ✧ *wisteria* ✧ *spoon* ✧ *indictment* ✧ *helix*

✧ *cavalry* ✧ *seal* ✧ *steeple* ✧ *fortnight* ✧ *smidgen*

Write the Story: **A New Customer Walks into the Shop**

Include the following in your story:

✧ *boudoir* ✧ *redwood* ✧ *west* ✧ *biography* ✧ *whiten*

✧ *sycophant* ✧ *mandatory* ✧ *commandment* ✧ *perform* ✧ *herbal*

Write the Story: **The Day Two Lifelong Friends Met**

Include the following in your story:

✧ *plantain* ✧ *greenhouse* ✧ *fleet* ✧ *premature* ✧ *lace*

✧ *possess* ✧ *divine* ✧ *culpable* ✧ *soulmate* ✧ *auspicious*

Write the Story: **A Team Comes Together**

Include the following in your story:

- ✧ *rugby*
- ✧ *mozzarella*
- ✧ *prism*
- ✧ *balsam*
- ✧ *channel*
- ✧ *puppet*
- ✧ *marvel*
- ✧ *quarrel*
- ✧ *contain*
- ✧ *parents*

Write the Story: **A Fan Fiction Writers' Group Meeting**

Include the following in your story:

✧ *hijack* ✧ *kiwi* ✧ *patience* ✧ *pendulum* ✧ *cunning*
✧ *leaden* ✧ *resign* ✧ *dawn* ✧ *fury* ✧ *mock*

Write the Story: **A Cabaret Singer's Night Off**

Include the following in your story:

✧ *kimono* ✧ *profound* ✧ *hypnotize* ✧ *caprice* ✧ *mutter*

✧ *custom* ✧ *oppress* ✧ *local* ✧ *cash* ✧ *unwittingly*

Write the Story: **Revisiting a Fond Memory**

Include the following in your story:

✧ *grief* ✧ *evidence* ✧ *covenant* ✧ *churn* ✧ *piazza*

✧ *intention* ✧ *vanish* ✧ *honeymoon* ✧ *careful* ✧ *crowd*

Write the Story: **A Second Chance**

Include the following in your story:

- *probation*
- *turbine*
- *pentagon*
- *renew*
- *flirt*
- *mindful*
- *dragonfly*
- *lukewarm*
- *hoot*
- *club*

Write the Story: **Scientists Are Never Off Duty**

Include the following in your story:

✧ *fossil* ✧ *reactor* ✧ *sage* ✧ *hell* ✧ *gluten*
✧ *devour* ✧ *fig* ✧ *landmine* ✧ *babble* ✧ *New Year*

Write the Story: **Nerds in a Heated Argument**

Include the following in your story:

✧ *tesseract* ✧ *synthesis* ✧ *padawan* ✧ *icebreaker* ✧ *chomp*
✧ *decipher* ✧ *utility* ✧ *keepsake* ✧ *slush* ✧ *croak*

Write the Story: **The Closing Arguments of a Big Case**

Include the following in your story:

✧ *courtroom* ✧ *wheelhouse* ✧ *catapult* ✧ *emit* ✧ *clamp*

✧ *peanut* ✧ *ticket* ✧ *vapor* ✧ *thimble* ✧ *decree*

Write the Story: **Retired Veterans Telling Their War Stories**

Include the following in your story:

✧ *internment* ✧ *fret* ✧ *kneel* ✧ *fasten* ✧ *drizzle*
✧ *nursery* ✧ *abundantly* ✧ *scarce* ✧ *discourteous* ✧ *grant*

Write the Story: **Old Friends Meet Over Coffee**

Include the following in your story:

✧ *Algonquin* ✧ *amazement* ✧ *elm* ✧ *tobacco* ✧ *hiss*

✧ *digress* ✧ *echo* ✧ *immense* ✧ *quiet* ✧ *opaque*

Write the Story: **Follow the Main Character Through a Day with No Dialog or Direct Interactions**

Include the following in your story:

✧ *sociopath* ✧ *buzz* ✧ *mend* ✧ *geyser* ✧ *awl*

✧ *consent* ✧ *diner* ✧ *second-hand* ✧ *vice* ✧ *wane*

Write the Story: **A Wedding Reception with Hundreds of Guests**

Include the following in your story:

✧ *war* ✧ *nag* ✧ *omit* ✧ *Ramadan* ✧ *downpour*

✧ *vouch* ✧ *loop* ✧ *gridlock* ✧ *allegro* ✧ *Filipino*

Write the Story: **The Hottest Day of the Year**

Include the following in your story:

- *suspense*
- *dogwood*
- *speculate*
- *playground*
- *peel*
- *avenue*
- *moderation*
- *classical*
- *yummy*
- *bluster*

Looking for more?

Similar titles available by Piccadilly:

300 Writing Prompts

300 MORE Writing Prompts

Sketch Your Sticker

Comic Sketchbook

300 Drawing Prompts

Calligraphy Made Easy

3000 Questions About Me

The Story of My Life

3000 Questions About My Future

500 Creative Prompts!

A Journey Within

The Fearless Woman

Church Notes

Complete the Story

Create + Destroy

Write the Poem

3000 Pick One Questions

Your Mother's Story

3000 What If? Questions

8-in-1 Sketchbook

Complete the Drawing